# Mindful Parenting for OCD Kids: Effective Guide to Helping your Child Manage OCD

Charles M. Jones

# Table of Contents


Chapter 1
Chapter 2
Chapter 3
Chapter 4
Chapter 5
Chapter 6

# Chapter 1

WHAT IS THIS OCD

What Is OCD, or Obsessive Compulsive Disorder?

Obsessive-compulsive disorder (OCD) is a mental illness characterized by persistent unfavorable thoughts or sensations (obsessions) or the need to do an action repeatedly (compulsions) (compulsions). Obsessions and compulsions may coexist in certain people.

OCD is not characterized by habits like nail-chewing or pessimistic thinking. An obsessional notion might be that certain colors or numbers are "good" or "bad." Washing your hands seven times after touching something that can be dirty might be considered an obsession. Even though you may not want to think or act in these ways, you find it difficult to stop.

Everyone has sometimes recurring behaviors or thoughts. OCD sufferers engage in or think about the following:

are uncontrollable, unpleasant, take up at least an hour a day, interfere with your career, your social life, or another aspect of your life.

Types of OCD and Symptoms

OCD may take many different forms, however, the majority of occurrences fall into at least one of four major categories:
Making assumptions about your health, such as that you have schizophrenia or pregnancy, or checking things like locks, alarm systems, stoves, or light switches. Contamination is a desire to clean or a fear of things that could be dirty. Feeling treated like garbage is what is meant by mental contamination.

The desire to arrange things in a certain way, together with symmetry and order. Ruminations, unwanted ideas, and a focus on a certain line of thought. Some of these concepts could be frightening or aggressive.

Having obsessions or compulsions
Many people with OCD are aware that their ideas and rituals are absurd. Instead of doing things because they like them, they do them because they are unable to stop. Furthermore, if they quit, they feel so bad that they restart.

Some examples of obsessive thinking are:

Fear of suffering harm to oneself or others.

persistent awareness of breathing, blinking, or other physical sensations.

the unfounded suspicion that a spouse is cheating but lack of evidence to support it.
Doing tasks in a certain order or a specific "good" number of times every time are examples of compulsive habits.
Must count stuff, such as steps or bottles aversion to using public restrooms, shaking hands, or touching doorknobs.

Causes of OCD and Risk Factors

Why some people acquire OCD is a mystery to medical professionals. Stress may worsen

symptoms. It affects women somewhat more often than men. Teenagers and young adults often experience the symptoms.
Risk factors for OCD include:

Having an OCD parent, sibling, or child variances in your brain's physical structure in certain areas.
anxiousness, tics, or depression.
Traumatized experience, a history of abuse as a child, either physically or sexually.

After a streptococcal infection, a kid may sometimes develop OCD. PANDAS, or pediatric autoimmune neuropsychiatric disorders associated with streptococcal infections, is the name used to describe them.

For OCD, there is no cure. With medicine, therapy, or a combination of treatments, however, you may be able to manage how your symptoms affect your life.

More specifically, obsessive-compulsive disorder (OCD) is a disease in which patients have recurring, undesirable thoughts, ideas, or sensations (obsessions), which push them to engage in repeated behaviors (compulsions) (compulsions). A person's daily activities and social relationships may be seriously hampered by repetitive behaviors like hand washing, checking on things, or cleaning.

Many people who do not have OCD suffer distressing thoughts or recurrent behaviors. These thoughts and actions, however, seldom interfere with daily life. OCD patients tend to have beliefs that stick with them and rigid behavior. Usually, considerable pain results from not doing the activities. Numerous OCD sufferers are aware of or feel that their obsessions are not useful; nonetheless, others may have inadequate awareness and consider their obsessions to be genuine (known as limited insight). People with OCD have problems letting go of their obsessive thoughts or stopping their compulsive behaviors, even when they are aware that their obsessions are unfounded.
OCD is characterized by obsessions and/or compulsions that are time-consuming (lasting more than an hour per day), distressing, and impair social or

occupational functioning. In the US, 2-3% of people have OCD, and among adults, women are affected more often than men. OCD often starts in infancy, adolescence, or early adulthood; the average age at which symptoms first show is 19.

Obsessions

Obsessions are persistent, recurrent thoughts, desires, or images that cause unpleasant emotions like fear or revulsion. Many OCD sufferers are aware of the excessive or unreasonable nature of their thoughts, impulses, or images and that they are the result of their brains. But neither reason nor logic can ease the suffering brought on by these invasive notions. Most OCD sufferers try to distract themselves from their obsessions, ignore or suppress them, or engage in other activities to minimize their suffering.

Usual Obsessions

apprehension about being contaminated by people or the environment

disturbing sexual images or ideas

Fear of yelling profanities or insults

extreme anxiety about precision, symmetry, or order

recurring, intrusive thoughts involving sounds, images, words, or numbers

Fear of misplacing or leaving something precious behind

Compulsions

Compulsions are repeated behavioral or mental behaviors that someone feels compelled to engage in as a result of an obsession. Often, the actions lessen or prevent an individual's pain brought on by an obsession. Compulsions may be excessive actions that are either directly connected to the obsession (such as excessive hand washing due to a fear of contamination) or completely unrelated to the fixation. In the worst situations, the day may be filled with routines that are repeated constantly, making it hard to go about your daily routine.

Regular Compulsions

Excessive or repetitive toileting, bathing, brushing teeth, or hand washing

Cleaning up after yourself repeatedly

organizing or arranging things in a certain way

repeatedly inspecting switches, locks, or equipment

persistently looking for affirmation or confirmation; repetitive counting to a predetermined quantity.

# Chapter 2

WHAT IS OCD NOT?

Many individuals mistakenly believe that OCD is just the slightly obsessive demand for order, cleanliness, and organization. There is some truth to this, and some OCD sufferers are preoccupied with these things, but not everyone's OCD manifests itself in the same way.

Beyond misconceptions about what OCD sufferers are like, people often blame mild OCD for their peculiarities and preferences. We may be very organized, and precise, and have preferred methods of doing things without having OCD. There are several instances of this:

maintaining a clean and well-organized space at all times.

storing just certain items in particular containers.
Placing specific objects, like shoes, in the same location each day and thinking that

you must get to work in the same manner are both signs of boredom.

being exacting while feeding others, making sure that they all get the same quantity.

People without OCD often exclaim, "I'm simply so OCD about this!" although this shows a lack of knowledge of the condition. OCD patients do have compulsions that are unique to them, but having "OCD about" one item is not a sign. These kinds of claims might increase people's misconceptions regarding the disease. These emotions may lessen the intensity of OCD while also allowing you to sympathize with others who do have it.

OCD is an obsessional personality disorder (OCPD)

Sometimes OCD is confused with OCDPD or obsessive-compulsive personality disorder. Although the conditions are quite distinct, the names are confusingly similar. While OCD is not a personality condition, OCPD is.

OCPD is often diagnosed in early adulthood and is characterized by an obsession with control, perfection, and orderliness in almost every aspect of an individual's life. Because they desire their houses to be spotless, people with OCPD may spend a lot of time cleaning them. They may keep their closets exceedingly neat and organized, and if their orderliness is disrupted, they could feel irritated. However, they don't feel worried about it; instead, they consider their actions and beliefs acceptable.

Others could consider the OCPD's actions "strange" or even upsetting. The effects of OCPD may harm a person's social interactions. It's not OCD, however. People with OCPD like the world as they have created it. People with OCD, on the other hand, are overpowered by the ideas and anxieties that enter their heads and don't enjoy what is occurring to them. They wish to quit performing compulsions but are unable to do so because of the intrusive thoughts, doubts, and desires that drive them.

More so, collecting things or being attracted to a specific subject of interest, such as stamps, coins, antiques, books by a favorite author, or even science fiction, fantasy, or cartoon memorabilia, does not fall within the definition of OCD. The pursuit of collectible objects gives collectors satisfaction, and they take pleasure in discussing or displaying their holdings to others.

Similar to this, sports fans may discuss their preferred sport or list many sports data. Interests in a topic that are normal and age-appropriate do not indicate the existence of OCD.

Fans who are apparently "obsessed" with celebrities, such as television or movie stars, well-known musicians, or members of professional sports teams, are not said to be the hallmark of OCD in older kids, teenagers, or adults.

Even if they appear to be "obsessed" with wanting to read every magazine article about their "idol," collect fan memorabilia, participate in Twitter and online blogs, and want to buy every CD, MP3, DVD, or video download of their favorite personality, kids and teenagers who have a "crush" on another person (especially a celebrity) do not have the crush because of OCD.

It's crucial to realize that misunderstandings concerning OCD may sometimes be caused by popular periodicals. Obsessive and/or compulsive disorders may be used to describe criminal and aggressive conduct. The word "obsessed" may be used to describe stalkers in articles that provide information about them. Such representations might result in erroneous and perhaps unpleasant ideas about what OCD sufferers are like.

Additionally, obsessive lying, shopping, gambling, or other actions that show a lack of impulse control are not signs of OCD. People with these issues may have diagnosable mental diseases, but OCD is not one of them.

The last distinction to make is between OCD and the peculiar patterns of interest shown by people with autism spectrum disorder, who have an all-encompassing concern with a specific, constrained interest that is either aberrant in intensity or concentration.

Incorrect usage of the labels "obsessive" and "compulsive" contributes to misconceptions about OCD and minimizes the actual pain that the condition may cause. People are increasingly referring to themselves as being "a little OCD" as the internet and social networking sites are utilized more often.

The term or diagnosis of obsessive-compulsive disorder, which may render a person incapacitated for hours at a time, is not appropriate for these obsessive or compulsive eccentricities, which last just a minute and seldom cause suffering or any concern.

Today's population seems to want to give every unique conduct a name, but when they refer to uncommon "obsessive" or "compulsive" behavior as "OCD," they are misrepresenting what it is. For instance, having an obsession with something fun like sports, shopping, sex, or any engaging activity is far different from having an obsession with something boring like OCD.

OCD also has nothing to do with people who collect items out of a particular passion, such as stamps, coins, books by a favorite author, or even mementos from sports or movies. Collectors like the quest for and purchase of the artifacts they are interested in, and they are delighted to discuss or display their collections to others. Hoarders with OCD, on the other hand, vary in that they often accumulate and hoard worthless, apparently useless items out of a worry that doing so would hurt them. Hoarders without OCD, on the other hand, are far from cheerful or proud.

When used about stalkers or "obsessed" fans, such as those who are allegedly "obsessed" with a particular person or celebrity, the word "obsession" has also come to connote something sinister. Of course, this is completely unrelated to obsessive-compulsive disorder and does not imply that an obsessed person has OCD.

# Chapter 3

OCD IN CHILDREN: THEIR EXPERIENCE

How Can OCD in Children Be Spot?
Adults who work with children, such as parents, teachers, and sports coaches, must be able to recognize any potential OCD symptoms in them. The greater the chance for a successful outcome at the outset of a mental health crisis, the sooner you can take action.

OCD is not associated with many common developmental rituals, such as sleep patterns. However, if a ritual starts to interfere with how a child behaves, it may be possible to tell if it's more than just a routine and might be a sign of OCD.

Often, OCD steadily worsens over time. Given the delayed onset of symptoms and a parent's innate desire to shield and console, it could be challenging for adults to recognize a child's OCD symptoms when they first appear.

The impact of OCD on children's and their environment's quality of life may be easier to observe.

There are many things to look out for that might be OCD symptoms.

The following are not always signs of OCD. These are examples of behaviors that might indicate that a child needs help from a knowledgeable adult and may be in distress.

Homework

OCD children could take an excessively long time to complete their schoolwork. Children may have to repeatedly read the same text, correctly write each number in a math problem, or check their schoolwork so many times that it takes a very long time to finish.

Away from the House

OCD children could make the family leave the house more slowly.

A child may check every door, window, and light to ensure they are in the "proper" settings or conditions before leaving, for instance, if they are taking their time to get ready. They can get upset if they have to leave before this activity is finished.

Because of this propensity, the family often arrives late for gatherings.

Handwashing

When it comes to OCD, handwashing is one of the most well-known compulsions.

A fixation with germs, feelings of revulsion, or other sorts of contamination, such as "bad emotions," or ideas of developing chronic tension, anxiety, or concern, maybe the source of handwashing. If handwashing and OCD are related, it can be wise to look for signs of raw, bleeding skin on the hands.

If children wash their hands often during the day, the soap will make the skin harsh and cause scars, skin peeling, and bleeding.

# Chapter 4

OCD MANAGEMENT

Drug or alcohol use

Children may turn to drugs as a coping mechanism sometimes when they are having trouble controlling a condition. Teens who are experiencing mental health issues might feel isolated from society, misunderstood, or overburdened. Sometimes, this results in drug misuse.

Sleep Routines. Bedtime or sleep problems are often caused by OCD. Before going to bed and drifting off to sleep, OCD children may need to follow a very specific routine. Additionally, if they have intrusive thoughts or anxiety that is worse at night, they could find it difficult to fall asleep. They must start the whole process again if this timetable is disturbed for any reason.

It is not unusual for OCD to have the evening procedure last for up to an hour. This deprives children of essential sleep, which has an impact on their ability to learn, their emotional growth, and their interactions with their peers and family members.

Regular sleep interruptions may also materially reduce the effectiveness of CBT and other OCD therapies.

Think about

There may be other ways for OCD to manifest in children than these behaviors. Additionally, it does not imply that if a child has difficulties with objects, they have OCD.

These are a few situations when a child could have unpleasant thoughts, feelings, or sensations and then engage in behaviors or avoid situations to feel better.

Parents may think about talking with a certified specialist about the possibility of OCD if this cycle of discomfort-relief causes family distress or disruption.

# Chapter 5

OCDE CAUSES

What Affects a Child's OCD?

There is often more than one reason for a child to acquire OCD, much like with other mental health disorders.

The following list of risk factors is by no means comprehensive, but it does provide a brief glimpse into what may help OCD develop. The fact that anybody might experience any kind of mental health issue, including OCD, must always be kept in mind.

History of the family, genetics, and environment
OCD is inherited. This implies that the likelihood of a child developing it is higher if someone in the family already has it. Although no specific genes have yet been linked to OCD, the familial pattern of OCD suggests that there may be a hereditary component to the disorder.

It is important to understand that the environment also plays a role when comparing nature vs. nurture. Over time, compulsions and obsessions may be taught. Children could pick up on similar behavioral habits if they see family members and others battle OCD. Environmental exposures may thus contribute to the development of OCD.

Tense situations

Children with OCD who may have underlying vulnerabilities may be in danger from stressful events. Children who experience trauma may develop PTSD, which is often mistaken for OCD.

While OCD and unwanted and intrusive thoughts (UITs) often concentrate on future uncertainty and attempt to reduce it, trauma focuses on intrusive thoughts based on the previous painful event. UITs are prevalent with trauma and post-traumatic stress disorder (PTSD) and may seem similar to OCD.

# Obsessive-compulsive disorder in children: are they just "little adults"?

# Chapter 6

Taking Care of Your Child's OC at Home

Define limits

While it is uncomfortable to see your child suffer, if you do not set boundaries, it will be more challenging for them to recover from OCD. For instance, a suitable response if your child tells you that you must change your clothes before entering their room is, "I know this is difficult for you, but this is just your OCD. Before I get to your room, I'm not going to change."

When you start setting limits regularly, your child will surely have a "meltdown" or an outburst, but they will also become used to your consistency. Setting boundaries will make your child feel less anxious over time.

Be Firm in your Approach

You must be very clear with your child that you are not allowing their OCD to dominate you and be sure to do as you say. Remind your child that the goal is not to harm or punish them, but rather to prevent OCD from controlling their lives or the lives of the family.

Being firm indicates that you will carry through your spoken promises to your child. For instance, if you inform them that the water will be turned off after 10 minutes, turn the water off at the appropriate time. It is vital to be clear and then act on your commitments.

Verify that your child's other caretakers use the same philosophy.

For a child with OCD, receiving consistent signals from all of their caregivers—both within and outside of their immediate family—is very essential. A child with OCD may become more stressed, perplexed, and insecure as a result of consistency.

Establishing your response and the responses of your child's other caregivers in advance of OCD scenarios is a smart idea. For instance, if your goal is to reduce a child's repetitive behavior, you can decide to let them repeat something three times. Each caregiver must follow through on this decision and decide on the consequences for their children if they disobey the rule. If one caregiver is more forgiving than the others, the child may become confused and cynical about the process. The system can then malfunction as a result of this disparity, feeding the OCD rather than reducing it.

Avoid accommodating or encouraging OCD

By accommodating OCD, you are participating in a child's rituals or changing your behavior to make them happen. With accommodations, maintaining a schedule that you deem essential is less important than not disturbing your child.

Accommodations might be made in:

Give your child ten kisses instead of one, let them take their cutlery out of the drawer and only use it for the dishes that are impacted, and change your clothes after your child warns you that they will be upset if you don't.

As a parent of an anxious child, you believe you must reassure, soothe, and provide a sense of security. Of course, you want to assist and safeguard a troubled child and, to the greatest extent possible, save her from suffering. However, trying to protect a child with an anxiety illness like obsessive-compulsive disorder from things that make them anxious could be harmful to the child. Unknowingly appeasing the condition and allowing it to rule your child's life by doing what comes naturally to a parent.

Because of this, parents have a surprisingly significant role in addressing children's anxiety issues. Exposure and response prevention, a kind of cognitive-behavioral therapy, is the gold standard in treating OCD in children. The goal of therapy is to gradually and methodically "expose" the child to her anxieties so that she will no longer be afraid of and avoid specific things or situations. "Response prevention" refers to not allowing the child to do rituals to manage phobias. Research has indicated that including parents in treatment and identifying them as "co-therapists" boosts effectiveness since parents become so invested in their children.

The Levels of Fear

In therapy, the child, parents, and therapist create a "fear hierarchy" in which they all recognize the terrifying situations, rate them on a scale of 0 to 10, and deal with each one at a time. For instance, a small child who is afraid of germs and being sick could repeatedly approach "contaminated" locations and objects until her fear subsides and she can tolerate the activity. The young child would begin with a low-arousal object, like touching clean towels, then progress to more difficult things, such as holding partially consumed food out of the trash.

Stopping the child from doing the action that helps to reduce the anxiety is referred to as response prevention. A man with a fear of germs, for instance, would have to forgo washing his hands after handling the doorknob or the garbage. Through gradual exposure, he discovers that what he "fears" often does not materialize, which opens the door for new learning. It also trains him to tolerate uncomfortable feelings.

Exercise at Home

CBT involves a lot of practice outside of sessions, therefore parents must participate in the treatment. Children are given "homework" and told to keep working on managing their anxiety in various situations. Family involvement and support are essential since exposure and response prevention produce anxiety and need extensive follow-up.

Parents may encourage a child who fears contamination to wash the dishes or to become a "human vacuum cleaner," which is what doctors refer to as picking up little pieces of trash from the carpet. In therapy, a small child who fears throwing up could create a comic about "Vomit Man" and practice reading it out to his parents.

The Consequences of Assurance

However, parents are more accountable than backup when it comes to home exposure training. Families typically get too preoccupied with a child's symptoms in an attempt to assist the child's function since OCD may be a paralyzing illness for youngsters. For example, a lot of kids with OCD and other anxiety problems need constant reassurance from their family members. Children use reassurance seeking to deal with their anxieties, and many parents provide it to their children—even when it's excessive—to help them feel better right now.

One of the many different sorts of "family accommodation" is assurance-seeking. This phenomenon is related to how family members participate in the rituals the child uses to manage his anxiety and how they modify their own and the family's routines to suit him.

Many OCD-affected kids find it difficult to deal with ambiguity and demand that their parents provide them with clear-cut answers. For instance, it is common to hear a frightened child ask their parents, even after receiving the answer many times, "Am

I going to get sick from eating this?" or "Is everything going to be okay?"

Parents may get easily agitated if they believe that no matter how many times their child's inquiries are answered, they will never be completely pleased. The parent's attempts to satisfy their child's questions spiral out of control, and the child is never taught that he can handle uncertainty.

Conciliating Fears

Numerous different types of accommodation are available. Families may forgo trips, forego dining out, or even alter their communication style to shield their kids from situations that may cause worry. Some names, numbers, colors, and sounds that make them anxious may be avoided.

This sounds all too similar to the family of Peter, a 12-year-old child who received OCD treatment at the Child Mind Institute. Peter worried about becoming sick and gaining weight, so he avoided eating anything considered to be "unhealthy," took up to seven showers each day, avoided playing with his brothers, and avoided hugging and kissing his parents out of fear that they were infected.

Peter's mother said, "We didn't go out to a restaurant for months." He did not have any friends visit. No one from our social circle visited us. We felt safe in our own house.

However, assuaging Peter's anxiety increased, it continued to rule his life more and more. The height of Peter's OCD was a very stressful time for her family, according to Peter's mother. Because it seemed like we had lost our child, it was very traumatic. He was so submerged in his OCD. We were unable to approach him directly. There was no longer any spontaneity. Even sitting across the table and conversing was no longer an option.

Anxiety Increasing

Although the parents who accommodate their children do so with good intentions, family accommodation is known to exacerbate the symptoms of the child. Since avoidance is how anxiety is maintained, family members who accommodate their children are assisting in the symptoms being even more fixed.

Peter's mother said, "I felt I was assisting even before I knew what accommodation was. "When I learned what accommodations were, it made me unhappy. The realization that I was aiding Peter's OCD rather than assisting him made me unhappy.

Naming the child's OCD is one way to lessen the stigma associated with it and to help the child understand that her nervousness is not who she is. For instance, a small child would refer to her OCD as "The Bully" or "The Witch." The separation of Peter's OCD from him has been substantial, Peter's mother says. Everyone in the family is now fighting the same enemy. A mysterious intruder was there before. We are aware of our adversary today.

Developing Adaptability

Through counseling, parents learn new strategies for responding to "stuck" children and how to encourage their children to use coping mechanisms or "boss back" their anxiety instead of depending on their parents to help them through it. The parents may begin to realize that concern no longer controls their families as the kids progressively become more independent.

However, they are often not involved in treatment as frequently as parents are. Grandparents and siblings may also participate in family accommodations.

Children's Fears and How to Help Them

Family members acquire the skills necessary to help their children face their fears rather than avoid them via treatment. Instead of calming the child, the parent's job is to remind him of the coping mechanisms he learned in therapy and to use them right now.

The Family's Function

It is clear that family members, especially extended family members, are deeply involved in OCD. Everyone is affected by a child's OCD and must cope with it. However, as a parent, you have the power to shape the dynamics of the household and encourage everyone - even extended family members - to support the OCD-stricken child.

For instance, let siblings know that the OCD child is actively trying to get well. Try to foster understanding and provide examples of how they might interact respectfully with their sibling or sister rather than retaliating angrily or in a derogatory manner. According to research, just being critical or harsh with family members might exacerbate OCD symptoms.

The Treatment Role of Parents

There are several ways that parents may influence their kids' behavior. You must thus encourage your child or teenager to seek out and participate in Cognitive Behavior Therapy (CBT) (CBT). You have the power to help or hinder your child's efforts to get OCD therapy.

The Power of Information

It may seem obvious, but the more you understand OCD and its treatment, the more equipped you'll be to help your child. We implore you to

Discover the signs and symptoms of OCD. Knowing OCD can help you see its warning signs and better understand the struggles your child has while battling this disorder. Discover CBT. The only behavioral treatment for OCD with scientific backing is this one, and experts in the field generally concur. In certain cases, CBT is combined with drug administration. As a result, it's a good idea to familiarize yourself with the challenges related to OCD medication.

Take Initiative in the Battle Against OCD

If OCD is not treated, it usually becomes worse. Making an explanation for actions your child does that might be signs of OCD won't help. Nor will they simply sit back and wait for your son or daughter to "grow out of it" or go through a phase. You'll significantly increase your child's chances of successfully regaining control over this potentially crippling condition by being proactive and taking action.

The Function of Families

Family members, especially extended family members, are deeply involved in OCD. Everyone is affected by and must cope with a child's OCD. However, as a parent, you have the power to shape how your household functions and to encourage everyone - even distant relatives - to support the OCD-stricken child.

For instance, let siblings know that the OCD child is actively trying to get well. Try to foster understanding and provide examples of how they might interact respectfully with their sibling or sister rather than retaliating angrily or in a derogatory manner. According to research, just being critical or harsh with family members might exacerbate OCD symptoms.

To be honest with everyone, nobody loves OCD, not even you. And especially not the child who is battling this condition. Encourage family members to make every effort to keep their irritation and contempt for the condition apart from the person who has it. The child's OCD is not his or her fault.

Families are often included by therapists in CBT. Research evaluating CBT for OCD in kids and teens showed that those whose families actively engaged in the therapy had some of the highest levels of recovery. Discuss with your child's therapist how you and your family may become involved in their treatment plan.

Parents must balance their worries about privacy with the potential benefits of having instructors assist their kids in overcoming OCD.

Whether or if you tell the teachers at your child's school about his or her OCD is ultimately up to you. Due to the stigma that is still commonly associated with mental illness, even in this day and age, some parents may not want to inform school officials about their son's or daughter's

OCD. In certain cases, parents worry that disclosing information to their child's teachers would breach their child's privacy.

But failing to inform school staff might result in further problems. First off, OCD symptoms often wax and wane (become worse before getting better) (get worse and then better). Therefore, there is always a potential that even if OCD symptoms aren't present at school right now, they may be there later on. If symptoms do become bothersome, teachers who are unfamiliar with the child may rely on faulty explanations and draw incorrect conclusions about those difficulties (e.g., the child is inattentive, noncompliant, rowdy, etc). (For instance, the youngster is oblivious, disobedient, rebellious, etc.) Because OCD behavior was seen to be aggressive or disruptive, students may face sanctions. Second, if a student is taking medication for OCD, school personnel should be made aware of the medicine's impact on a student's behavior, including any potential side effects. Teachers who are aware of a student's OCD are better able to grasp their conduct and provide the support that is necessary for a student to perform well in school.

www.ingramcontent.com/pod-product-compliance
Lightning Source LLC
Chambersburg PA
CBHW051936150726
47999CB00006B/2244